GW01460182

Reformation's Rib

celebrating
Katherine von Bora

James G. Cobb

CSS Publishing Company, Inc., Lima, Ohio

REFORMATION'S RIB

For more information about CSS Publishing Company resources, visit our website at
www.csspub.com.

ISBN 0-7880-1832-9

PRINTED IN U.S.A.

To Ellen Wingard Cobb and James Kivett Cobb, my parents, whose parsonage life was my refuge and strength, and descended from those early, first Protestant parsonages.

To my wife Judith A. Cobb (The Reverend) who has made our parsonage life and marriage and family a joy and a worthy descendent of Katie and Martin's life together.

Reformation's Rib is a drama/reading about The Reformation in honor of the 500th anniversary of the birth of **Katherine von Bora**, b. 1499 - d. 1550, wife of Martin Luther.

The text is based largely on two books by Roland Bainton:
Here I Stand: A Life Of Martin Luther (Abingdon-Cokesbury Press, New York, Nashville, 1950).
Women Of The Reformation (Augsburg Publishing House, Minneapolis, 1971).

The history and story collected in these books are also from previous histories, biographies, and translated works listed as primary sources in the two books. Additional consulted sources include:
Luther's Works: Table Talk, Volume 54 (Fortress Press, Philadelphia, 1967), Helmut T. Lehmann, General Editor.
What Luther Says, an anthology (3 volumes) (Concordia Publishing House, St. Louis, 1959), Edward M. Plass, Compiler.
Luther Lives! (CSS Publishing, Lima, Ohio, 1983), John R. Brokhoff.

Also, the writer must cite lectures, conversations, and classes with the Reverend Dr. Eric Gritsch, Professor Emeritus, Reformation History, Lutheran Theological Seminary, Gettysburg, Pennsylvania, a world-renowned Luther Scholar and my mentor, to whom I am forever grateful.

And my thanks to Ruth C. Gritsch, friend, mentor, and translator of *Luther's Works*.

Reformation's Rib:
Celebrating Katherine von Bora

Characters:
Narrator
Katie Luther
Martin Luther
(Script may be read, though dramatic interpretation, even memorization heightens the effect)

Costumes:
Martin Luther: black robe
Katie Luther: large, gray or dark medieval dress, simple and unadorned

Staging:
Narrator: at a pulpit or lectern to one side
Martin and Katie: standing or sitting in simple living room
(Spotlight on each character as they speak is helpful. Martin and Katie are usually in dialogue and can be spotlighted together.)

Narrator: The reformation of Christendom exploded on the scene October 31, 1517, when an Augustinian monk named Martin Luther proposed 95 theses for debate within the Roman Catholic Church. You most probably know the rest of the history: reforms of the Church were popular with much of the German public and were summarily condemned by Church authorities. By the 1520s a religious conflagration engulfed Europe. The Church of the Reformation was called "Lutheran" by its enemies and "Evangelical" or Gospel-centered by its supporters. Doctrines and teachings were newly exposed to the light of critique; Scripture was central to the Church again; music and liturgy enjoyed a renaissance; parishes experienced new energies, life, and vitality with hymn-singing, and the language of the Church corresponded to the language of the people. And, for us in Protestant churches, parsonage life was introduced as former priests and nuns entered into sometimes arranged marriages and continued service in the church's life. And thus there comes the story of Katherine von Bora, the former nun who married Martin Luther. How did that happen? What would that mean?

Katie: I was born in January, 1499. At the age of ten, my widowed father decided to re-marry and a young daughter no longer fit his plans. Father placed me in a convent in Nimchen. Ten years old I was. I took my Holy Order vows at sixteen. (*Pauses reflectively*) In the 1520s our convent began to read tracts and treatises of the Reformation, especially the writings of a monk named Martin Luther. Nine of us sisters were quite drawn to the reform proposals. Together we wished to escape the convent and lend support to the new movement. We made plans to make a secret escape from our convent. The threat of condemnation and death was very real.

Martin: Many former priests and nuns joined the movement for church reform. Our thoughts turned to necessary precautions for their protection, and sometimes a plan for their departure away from persecution. Churches aligning with the reform movement needed priests and nuns to serve as they had previously. Re-assignment to congregations was one option. If these priests and nuns resided in the territory of Frederick the Wise in Saxony, all was well. They were free. But if they resided in the region of Duke George, their very lives were in danger should they support the reformation. But — we had a plan. We heard (*whispers*) very confidentially of the wish of nine nuns to leave the convent of Nimchen. A friend named Leonard Kopp delivered barrels of smoked herrings to the convent by wagon.

Katie: One Easter night, it was proposed that Leonard Kopp's wagon not return to Wittenberg with empty barrels but with a wagon load of escaping nuns! And this he did! And it worked!

Martin: Nuns were placed in various homes of parishioners. Over a couple of years, marriages were arranged, sometimes between former priests and nuns. I could find no Scripture prohibition. Why, indeed, it quite clearly states that our Lord healed the mother-in-law of Peter. Marriage is a natural estate begun by our Lord in the Garden of Eden. Why should the Church suggest a prohibition to its servants? Anyway, the Reformation helped make new lives for its leaders and servants. Most went along rather smoothly with arrangements. But then I personally heard of one nun's protest. One Katherine von Bora said this to me ...

Katie: Dr. Luther, I will *not* marry Dr. Glatz! That's that! No!

Martin: "Who then?" I asked. I saw her cut her eyes! Me? No, it's impossible. Immediately through my mind ran a scenario of danger. I would later write to a friend, "If I am burned at the stake as a heretic, I am afraid Katie would suffer the same fate." I knew that with the posting of the papal ban, I could be burned to ashes, and my life was fraught with danger. Danger for me lurked like shadowy devils at every turn.

Narrator: When Katie balked at other matrimonial suggestions, she made a proposal of her own. She would marry either of the two "older" Reformation leaders: either Amsdorf or Luther. Luther finally understood this as a serious ultimatum. Luther gave the

7

idea new consideration. In June, 1525, he had heard that Albert, the archbishop of Mainz, against whom the 95 theses had been directed, was himself contemplating marriage. Luther thought such an idea might be right. Thus, on June 13, 1525, the couple was married in the presence of four witnesses. Two weeks later, the public joined in a grand celebration with parades, music, and a great and large banquet. Luther's parents were especially pleased. Luther would later state that he married for three reasons ...

Martin: For these reasons, I married: to spite the pope, kick the devil, and please my father!

Katie: (*Sarcastically*) Thank you, Doctor Luther!

Martin: Dear Katie, please remember that the very idea of romantic love had not yet come along. These modern notions held by this audience today were not part of our thinking in the sixteenth century. In our day, a couple first exchanged a promise of their covenant, then ... they hoped, love would be experienced and enjoyed.

Katie: Then, I must ask, Dear Doctor, what would you say about me later, after the vows?

Martin: Dear Katie: I told many a colleague that life greatly changed for me when I rolled over in bed and found a pair of pigtails on my pillow.

Narrator: Indeed, life did change. Luther's letters through the years would say these things:

Martin: "I would not exchange Katie for France or for Venice, for God has given her to me, and other women have worse faults. She has a few, but her virtues outweigh them." And I wrote ...
   "My wife is agreeable, accommodating and affable beyond anything I dared to hope. I would not exchange my poverty for the riches of Croesus." And this ...

8

"If I were to lose my Katie, I would not take another wife though I were offered a queen."

Narrator: Luther often called Katie "the morningstar of Wittenberg," and we think this is reference to her rising at 4 a.m. in the summer and 5 a.m. in the winter to oversee a household of large numbers. In terms of his wife's management, Luther wrote:

Martin: "I seem so often to rely more on Katie than on Christ. In domestic matters I defer to Katie; in all others things, I am led by the Holy Spirit."

Narrator: Katie was a good and worthy partner for her famous husband. She was well educated and could answer him in Latin as well as their native German. Yet, even in the sixteenth century, a famous person's family might be the brunt of rumor and gossip and personal attack. Katie was once the subject of a pamphlet's ridicule.

Katie: It was hurtful to pick up a tract directed at me. I shall never forget its words: "Woe to you, poor fallen woman, not only because you have passed from light to darkness, from the cloistered holy religion into a damnable, shameful life, but also that you have gone from the grace to the disfavor of God, in that you have left the cloister in lay clothes and have gone to Wittenberg like a chorus girl. You are said to have lived with Luther in sin. Then you have married him, forsaking Christ your bridegroom. You have broken your vow and by your example have reduced many godly young women in the cloisters to a pitiable state of body and of soul, despised of all men." After reading such lies I must tell you that I loved Martin all the more when he said to dismiss such garbage as I would if I were kicking the devil!

Narrator: Luther's affection for Katie was ever on the increase. He referred to her first as "my lady." Then, "my lord," and later, when she also managed a country farm two days' ride from Wittenberg, he called her, "my rich lady of Zulsdorf." In letters to

9

friends, he would say, "I and my rib send greetings to you and your rib." Towards the end of his life, Luther wrote a letter to her addressed, "To my dear wife, Katherine von Bora, preacher, brewer, gardener, and whatever else she may be." Many roles fell to Katie in her married life, none more pleasing than the role of "mother."

Katie: Martin and I had six children. When we were married, the elector Frederick gave us a former monastery called the "black cloister" for our home. It had over forty rooms! They seemed always to be filled, first with our family, then with university students, then with my aunt and various other relatives from time to time. Foreigners came calling to meet and converse with the famous Dr. Luther. We were a hostel for religious refugees from all over Europe. We coined your modern phrase, "Guess who's coming to dinner?" This great building in Wittenberg contained three cellars, a bath, a laundry, and a good brewery for German beer. I saw to a garden, an orchard, another garden with a brook and pond for fish. We had livestock including eight pigs, five cows, nine calves, chicken, geese, and one dog named Tolpel, which in German, means "blockhead." I can say I herded, milked, slaughtered, made butter and cheese, brewed, fished, planted, harvested, and recruited a small army of helpers and workers needed for this sprawling mass of humanity! All in all, I still say that Dr. Luther, though a father-figure to many, was a good father in this family unit we called home. Still, one could not erase all his former monastic training. In his fastidious nature to make all clothing last, he would sew a patch on his torn breeches. Only one problem: his patch came from another pair of breeches still in use by his son, Hans!

Martin: Please, do not be so hard on me, dear Dr. Katie.

Narrator: The Luthers were parents to six children. The first, Hans, was born June 7, 1526. At the birth of this son, Luther said:

Martin: "My dear Katie brought into the world yesterday by God's grace, at two o'clock, a little son, Hans Luther. I must stop. Sick

Katie calls me." When the baby was bound in swaddling clothes, I said, "Kick, little fellow. That is what the pope did to me, but I got loose."

Narrator: Their second child, a daughter, lived less than a year. Of the four remaining, Magdalene, Martin, Paul, and Margareta, Magdalene died at age fourteen. Perhaps her father's favorite, it was a dark time for her parents.

Martin: At her deathbed, I held her and spoke, "My dear Lenchen, you would like to stay here with your father *and* you would be glad to go to your Father in heaven? She said, 'Yes, dear father, as God wills.' " She died in my arms. (*Pauses*) I must tell you, I could not find it in my heart to give God thanks. Katie sobbed in a corner of the room. At her grave I said, "Dear child: you will rise and shine like the stars and the sun." How strange it is to know that she is at peace and all is well and yet to be so sorrowful.

Katie: Martin and I shared many joys and also many griefs. After Lenchen's death, Martin addressed his congregations and said, "I must be away from you for a while. Please continue to say the prayers and speak the Creed and sing the hymns and I shall rejoin you when I can" ... God and time and friends helped us. (*Pauses*)
Let me continue the story ... the man could lose himself in work. Think what you moderns say of him: in 1983, on the occasion of the five hundredth anniversary of his birth, scholars would write, "More has been written by or about Martin Luther than any other person in recorded history except Jesus." Can you imagine such an assessment? His writings were by the sun's light or by candle light ... with quill pen and ink well (no copiers or computers or spell check or keyboards). Think of his writings: they fill over fifty volumes from notes students made at table, and then there are his lectures and sermons, tracts and treatises. The man had energy and scholarship and passion for Jesus and his Church! And he had love for his wife and children and students and relatives and friends too numerous to know.

11

Narrator: Modern medicine might speculate about tendencies of energy bursts and slow-down times. We might hypothesize about some cyclic manic/depressive swings for Luther. Katie would not know the terms but could describe some of the occasions, times when Martin seemed despondent and distant.

Katie: Doctor Luther had been in a despondent, sad mood for much too long. I don't recall if there was reason for such a mood but I decided on a course of action. I dressed in black (*dons a black shawl or hat*) ... and met him at the door.

Martin: Katie, you are in the color of mourning. Who died?

Katie: I spoke what I felt: "Your God died. At least, so you act!" I suppose it was dramatic for me, but I think the shock of my words and actions did succeed. We did get him back and that was the point. When he could do some self-evaluation, he wrote:

Martin: "Don't try to self-help your way through such times. Don't argue with the devil. He's had 7,000 years of experience. He has tried out his trickery on Adam, Abraham, and David, and he knows exactly the weak spots. And he is persistent. If he does not get you down with the first assault, he will commence a siege of attrition until you give in from sheer exhaustion. Better banish the whole subject. Seek company and discuss some irrelevant matter, as for example, what is going on in Venice. Shun solitude. Eve got in trouble when she walked in the garden alone. I have my worst temptations when I am by myself. Seek out some Christian, some wise counselor. Undergird yourself with the fellowship of the Church. Then, too, seek convivial company, feminine company; dine, dance, joke, and sing. Make yourself eat and drink, though food may be very distasteful. Fasting is the very worst expedient."

Katie: Martin once gave three rules of advice for dispelling despondency (and he should know): first is faith in Christ; the second is to get downright angry; third is the love of a spouse. Good advice, then and now? I think so. (*Pauses*) I think there was another medicine for Dr. Luther. It was his visitation to parishioners. It went back to April, 1521. Dr. Luther entered the city of Worms to face one of the greatest ordeals of his life. There was a rousing demonstration. He fell into bed nearly dead with fatigue. He was scheduled to appear the next afternoon at the Diet. What did he do? Did he go over speeches and outlines? Did he research biblical texts or church fathers? Did he agonize in prayer? Tell the people what you did.

Martin: I visited a dying man in that town. He had requested that I come. I heard his confession and administered the sacrament. And when I glimpsed again the power of the gospel in this ministry, I knew that no power on earth could stand against the faith of even a weak and dying old man.

Katie: Reports said that Martin Luther entered the great hall in quiet calm and at peace with a smile on his face.

Martin, as you might guess, was a people person: gregarious, bawdy, a noble scholar of peasant stock. We laughed a lot. One student at table told him once that a neighboring priest was conducting a graveside funeral when a dog walked up and relieved itself in the pot of holy water. The priest was reported to have shouted, "You impious dog! Are you a Lutheran too?"

There were times when I thought Dr. Luther too gregarious. Once he was at table, holding forth in an animated conversation, and was quite full of himself, arguing his position, and no one could manage an interruption until I butted in with a suggestion, "Doctor, why don't you stop talking and eat?" That gave him occasion to say:

Martin: "I wish that women would repeat the Lord's Prayer before opening their mouths."

Katie: Well, I in turn wish that men who were so full of their own pomp and position would catch the many hints that other people do prefer dialogue to monologue! Dr. Luther, you know, could be somewhat irritating! I once asked, "Dear Doctor, is the Prime Minister of Prussia the Duke's brother?" Martin responded:

Martin: "All my life is patience. I must have patience with the pope, with the heretics, with my family, and with my Katie."

Katie: Was that a compliment or dubious company? (*Pauses*) I must tell you: never did I doubt Martin's love. Once officiating at a wedding, Dr. Luther gave loving admonition to a couple and I heard his charge to them as his personal creed of marriage. To the groom he said, "Dear sir, make your wife sorry to see you leave the home each day." To the bride he said, "Dear woman, make your husband glad to re-enter your home."

I so cherish the memories of Martin as father to our children. He saw the family as the place to practice the Christian faith. At Christmas, he walked across the fields, saw stars between the boughs of evergreen trees, cut one down, and hauled it into our house to say, "This can teach us something of this season. There was a tree in the Garden of Eden and one we call the cross. One was our fall and one was our redemption. Let us decorate the tree with apples to remember the temptations and with candles to proclaim our Savior's birth as the light of the world." That was it: he gave us Christmas trees. And he wrote the small catechism, and I think it was with our children in mind. And he wrote music. Much of it was first hummed in our home. His hymn verses tell the story of our faith. He took a college song and wrote verses telling the whole narrative of Jesus' birth. You call it by the title, "From Heaven Above To Earth I Come." (*Pauses*) There is more I could tell. I have memories stored in heart and head, but God alone knows it all.

Martin: Before we leave, I wish to say it again, "Thank you, God, for giving me Katie. Thank you for our life and partnership together. Thank you for children to laugh and play and learn and grow at our hearth. Thank you for love in our marriage and for our faithful vows to one another. My dear Katie is wonderful and beautiful. Her occasional obstinant ways are born of character and conviction and courage and caring for me and our children and your

14

dear Church." My dear Katie: though death will be cruel and finally separate us, I will want you to know that I wrote a verse of tragic anticipation when I said a time would come when we would each know that the enemy of God would "take our house, goods, honor, child, and spouse, and our very life would be wrenched away." But you, Katie, and I know that one little word means they cannot win the day. That little word is Jesus our Lord. With our God and weapons of the Spirit, the Kingdom is ours forever! Thank you for sharing that with me, dear Doctor Katie.

Katie: And I would thank you, dear Doctor Luther, Martin, you wonderful servant of God, decisive and resolved to stand for the truth of the gospel and the freedom of grace. You are a champion of a just cause. Through you, truth does abide. You have defended and upheld God's grace given in Jesus as the One great Word the world must hear and hold dear and true. At night, I saw you cradle and rock your child in your arms while humming a new hymn for the church. I saw you lost in thought and writing but then stop to encourage our children in their play and frolic. Thank you, truly, dear Martin, for hosting the world in our home, and for your look of innocence when I motioned my disbelieving question to you, "How many for dinner?" Dear Dr. Luther: I feel complete and fulfilled in the life we shared together. I thank you, dear Doctor, as I thank our God. Thank you for how you have so helped us to pray: "Lord, keep us steadfast in your Word; curb those who by deceit or sword would wrest the kingdom from your Son and bring to naught all he has done."

Martin: "Lord Jesus Christ, your power make known, for you are Lord of lords alone; defend your holy Church, that we may sing your praise triumphantly."

Katie: "O Comforter of priceless worth, send peace and unity on earth; support us in our final strife and lead us out of death to life."

(*The hymn may be played as the two exit and before lights are turned on again*)

15

9 780788 018329